Selling Your Book

Selling Your Book

A Step-by-Step Guide
for Promoting and Selling Your Book

BRUCE E. MOWDAY

Published by Barricade Books Inc.
Fort Lee, NJ 07024

www.barricadebooks.com

Manufactured in the United States of America
Library of Congress Cataloging-in-Publication Data

Names: Mowday, Bruce E., author.
Title: Selling your book : a step-by-step guide for promoting and selling your book / Bruce E. Mowday.
Description: Fort Lee, NJ : Barricade Books Inc., [2017] | Includes bibliographical references and index.
Identifiers: LCCN 2017021719 | ISBN 9781569802229 (pbk. : alk. paper) | ebook ISBN 9781569808214
Subjects: LCSH: Books--Marketing. | Authorship--Marketing.
Classification: LCC Z285.6 .M69 2017 | DDC 002.068/8--dc23
LC record available at https://lccn.loc.gov/2017021719

2017021719

Contents

Foreword

If anyone knows how to market books, it's Bruce Mowday. He's an expert at promoting his books and reaching his readers.

Bruce uses the personal approach. He connects not only with individual readers but also groups. His presentations have been so successful, some groups have asked him back on multiple occasions.

The results of his unique marketing approach is evident. He is highly successful at marketing and selling his books.

The first time Barricade Books worked with Bruce was on his *Jailing the Johnston Gang: Bringing Serial Murderers to Justice*. Bruce said he could sell his book and I told him to go ahead. He did!

He's achieved excellent sales with his other books for Barricade, including:

> *Pickett's Charge: The Untold Story*
> *Why the Hall Not: Richie Ashburn's Amazing Journey to Cooperstown*
> *Life With Flavor: A Personal History of Herr's*
> *Jailing The Johnston Gang, Bringing Serial Murderers To Justice.*

Carole Stuart, Publisher
Barricade Books
April 2017

Acknowledgments

Contributions to this book have been made by countless people during the past decade. I've worked with a number of authors on marketing issues and I've studied the motivations of the book-buying public. Everyone I've met, knowingly or unknowingly, contributed to this marketing guide for authors.

Carole Stuart, publisher of *Barricade Books*, urged me to write an updated marketing guide for authors. My first marketing book for authors, *The Selling of an Author*, was published more than a decade ago. Carole has been a great supporter of my works and I deeply appreciate everything she has done to publish and promote my works. Carole is a wonderful publisher and published my books, *Jailing the Johnston Gang: Bringing Serial Murders to Justice*, *Why the Hall Not: Richie Ashburn's Amazing Journey to Cooperstown* and *Life With Flavor: A Personal History of Herr's*.

The information for this marketing book comes from personal experiences and taking part in many interesting discussions with fellow authors. We all seem to have common marketing issues, challenges and concerns. I was one of the founders of the Brandywine Writers Group because of the common issues facing authors. I thank all of the authors who have entered into these discussions with me over the years.

Author Charlene Briggs, who wrote a wonderful book about her father and World War II, has been very helpful in discussing many marketing aspects that involved reaching the right audience for her book.

The same appreciation goes to Matty Dalrymple. She is the author of the Ann Kinnear suspense novels. Matty and I have been involved in several seminars for authors and she has an excellent insight into the marketing process. She is great at developing niche marketing venues. Many times I joined her for events after Matty set up a series of signings at varied locations, including wineries.

Author and publisher Norman Mawby is thanked for his positive comments about this book. Norm has published two admirable books on baseball. I worked with Norm on both of the books. I was a contributing writer on one of the books and a marketing consultant on both of them.

Once again, Katherine Harlan was an excellent proofreader and has saved me from many of my mistakes. She has done the same for many of my books. Her work is greatly appreciated.

I also want to acknowledge all of the readers who have taken an interest in my books over the years and have given me valuable feedback.

The writing and promotion of a book is never an easy task.

Bruce E. Mowday
April 2017

Introduction

DON'T BLINK. The publishing world is rapidly changing. Authors need to continually adjust their marketing plans to fit the rapid modifications taking place in the publishing world. A few words of caution about my marketing ideas, I'm a non-traditionalist. You won't find many of these suggestions in the marketing plans you purchase for large sums of money from self-publishing companies.

Authors believing the way to sell books is to just list them on internet sites and sit in book stores waiting to sign copies for patrons are missing great opportunities to sell books. That's not my strategy.

All of the many industry changes have made an author's job much more difficult in every department, including writing, publishing, promotion and marketing. True, now anyone can be an author. The only requirement is finding funding for the pay-to-print world of self-publishing and vanity press.

Becoming a successful author is not so easy. Selling books is difficult for authors using a traditional publisher or delving into self-publishing. Without proper marketing, significant sales of books won't be attained. The competition is too stiff for an author to hope readers will find his book on the over-crowded internet bookshelf. And, without marketing books don't find their way into the remaining book stores across the country.

Finding a traditional publisher or agent is much more difficult in the current publishing world. There are fewer traditional publishers publishing fewer books than a decade ago. Making money in the publishing industry is extremely difficult, a fact authors need to keep in mind. Agents are looking for established authors. If their clients aren't selling books, the agents aren't making money.

Selling Your Book is intended for authors who want to be successful by marketing their own books with or without the aid of a traditional publisher. The target audience for this book is authors who don't have an immediately recognizable name by a large percentage of the world's population or a large national or international following.

While the internet and publishing services have made it easier to become an author, the same world has made selling books enormously more difficult. With Amazon listing more than 11 million books, the competition for sales is fierce. There is too much competition for authors to not be marketers.

I haven't met an author who secretly doesn't want to make millions of dollars from his book, secure a movie deal and live the fictitious life of a writer whose days are spent effortlessly creating fabulous prose, reading fawning fan e-mails and cashing large royalty checks.

Sorry, that's not the real world for 99 percent of

today's authors. Becoming a successful author is hard work involving the investing of a lot of time and wisely spending marketing dollars. Someone once said producing writing that is easy to read is hard work. That it is.

A writer's work doesn't end when a copy of a book is in the publisher's hands. An author's ability to promote, market and sell books will impact the number of books sold.

I have contact with authors who complain they have boxes of their books sitting in their basements and bedrooms and can't sell them. Other authors ask me why their books sell only a few copies a month despite being offered for sale on a myriad of internet platforms and outlets. Many of the non-traditional self-published authors admit they never come close to recouping their publishing investment.

The reality is writing a book is hard work and selling a book is harder work. The foundation of success is built upon having a good book to sell. Sales will be minimal if the book is poorly written, edited, produced and has a limited number of people interested in the subject. Authors of such books may be able to entice some buyers to purchase a copy but eventually sales will cease.

There are good reasons why the average number of books a title sells is less than 200 copies. That isn't a mistake. Authors will starve if their gross book sales are about $5,000 dollars. Remember book stores, publishers, distributors, editors and other sundry editorial services take a large part of that gross sales amount. Authors are at the bottom of the list to be paid.

Authors need to be smart marketers. Those authors who follow the traditional, conservative route of selling books—that is by sitting in a book store waiting for someone to purchase a book or waiting for a small royalty check—will soon realize that being an author can be an expensive hobby.

Writers have many sound reasons for writing books and I encourage them all to do so. Writing can be good for the soul even if the work is never published. Family histories are important as are local histories. Books entertain and enlighten readers and keep some authors sane.

Writers should have realistic expectations and a grasp of the publishing world before starting their endeavors. I've never been involved in a project that has smoothly sailed through the research, writing, publishing, distribution and sales phases of a book venture. There are obstacles, some small and some large, to overcome with every book.

Why should you spend your time reading this book and following the advice? Good questions. Authors will be offered many expensive services to publish and market books. Explore each offering before investing.

This book is drawn from my personal experiences.

The first time I was paid to write professionally was while I was in high school. I covered sports for a daily newspaper. That was 50 years ago. I spent more than two decades writing for daily newspapers. I've worked for magazines and have done hundreds of freelance articles. I'm still contributing editor to *Business 2 Business* magazine based in central Pennsylvania. For a brief period, I was co-publisher of a magazine. I've hosted three radio shows, including one of the first internet radio shows, and I guest host for a radio station.

I've appeared on *Discovery ID* channel, *C-SPAN* and a number of times on *Pennsylvania Cable Network* and local and regional television shows.

As for the books, in the past 20 years I've authored or contributed to 25 published books. They have gross sales of more than $1 million. I have sold many of the books myself, often one book at a time. As a tag line on my e-mails, I use *One More Book.* One more book to read, write and sell. If you check my BookScan numbers you won't be impressed. That is because a vast majority of my sales are not recorded by BookScan.

BookScan keeps track of books sold through traditional outlets, such as bookstores and internet sites. While I want to sell every book I can through those sources, I seek out venues where I can sell directly to readers. I once asked a publisher the following question. Why should I spend three hours in a bookstore, selling 30 books and wait six months for a royalty statement for maybe $30 when I can go to a local event that won't register on BookScan, sell the same number of books and walk home with $600 that amounts to about a $300 profit?

I didn't receive an answer to that question.

The key to my book selling success is I invest lots of time and effort into being available for interviews, book signings and book talks. I'll do more than 60 appearances a year and some years, especially when a new book is released, I'll do more than 80 events.

Authors are their own best marketing tool. Authors need to be enthusiastic about their books. They need to believe in their books. They must convince the book-buying public to purchase their books. If authors aren't excited about their books, no one else will be. On the downside, authors can be their worst marketing tool. A bad attitude will discourage readers and cripple book sales.

More than a decade ago, before the internet changed our lives, I wrote a marketing book for authors. While many of the basic marketing and business aspects of being an author have remained the same, the way authors reach potential book buyers has greatly changed. My first book dealt with press releases and bookstores, both fading into antiquity. This book embraces the world of social media. Social media has wonderful avenues for promotion. Social media also requires time and effort to be used effectively.

Remember, the publishing world is changing as we speak. Authors need to be aggressive non-traditionalists in the marketing world.

Bruce E. Mowday
April 2017

Chapter 1

IN THIS CHAPTER:

- ✧ Overcoming shyness
- ✧ Understanding the business of being an author
- ✧ Marketing is everything
- ✧ The importance of book titles and covers

Being just a writer won't lead to book sales in today's world. The mindset of an author needs to be adjusted. Authors need to develop new skills. Understanding the business side of publishing is the first step.

Chapter 1

Authors As Marketers

I'm an author. *I'm a writer. I'm an intellectual dilettante. I'm not a business person. I'm not a marketer. I'm not a salesperson. I'm not an entertainer. I'm an author.*

Sorry, a successful author is a business person, marketer, salesperson and entertainer. The only way an author can escape the business side of publishing is to have lots of money, or a patron with deep pockets, to finance a book. Few patrons of the arts exist today.

The writing of a book is a lonely pursuit. Writing is not a team sport. After a draft manuscript is completed, authors can seek out comments and constructive suggestions. During the creation of the manuscript, authors are on their own. Interruptions from friends, family members and the pet cat are not kindly tolerated when the prose is flowing. A movie made many years ago was titled *The Loneliness of a Long Distance Runner*. The writing process could be called *The Loneliness of an Author*.

So, how do I, an introverted author, become an extrovert once my book is published? I feel more secure locked in my office with my computer and a pot of coffee or a Keurig machine for the modern writers.

For many authors, the transition is not easy. As with any learned skill, an author will become more relaxed and proficient with experience. Recently I took part in a post-play audience participation program at the Peoples Light and Theatre Company in Malvern, Pennsylvania. I was a member of a panel discussing that night's play. My book *Pickett's Charge: The Untold Story* connected with the theme of the play.

I sat on stage with the other panel members as we gave comments about the production and fielded questions from the audience. I was asked to be the first panelist to talk to the audience since I've been speaking before groups for years. A friend told me I looked at ease before the large live audience. The questions weren't submitted in advance. I was at ease but the lack of stage fright wasn't innate. I remember my middle school teacher was hesitant to place me on a panel because I was so quiet in class. I never spoke or joined in class discussions. I was a classic introvert and in many ways I remain one.

Won't the publisher market my book?

If an author has a traditional publisher, the publisher will provide some marketing assistance. The publisher is in the business to sell books. There is a limit to assistance authors receive. Remember, publishers have a good idea as to the amount of money a book will generate. They also know how much money it will cost to produce, distribute, market and sell a book. Traditional publishers do have in-house marketing departments but authors shouldn't expect the publishers' marketing department to spend an inordinate amount of time working on their individual book.

My first book was about Fort Delaware during the Civil War. A respected historical publisher released the work. The publisher had a specific amount of money set aside for marketing. Ads were purchased in Civil War publications touting the book and placement was timed to match the release of the book. During the final phase of editing, the book's editor left the company to take another job. The release of the book was delayed a full year while another editor took over the project. The publishing house didn't purchase additional advertisements. The marketing budget was depleted. My co-author Dale Fetzer and I were left with the major marketing responsibilities. We weren't happy with the situation as the delay cost us initial sales. Even though we were disappointed with the book's launch, we persevered and did a number of signings and talks. The book was successful and still sells today.

UNDERSTAND THE BUSINESS OF BOOKS

Unless your book is expected to generate huge profits, don't expect publishers to finance a book tour across the world, the country, your state or even to the neighboring town. Book tours are expensive and publishing is a business where the bottom line is being squeezed. Authors need to understand the business side of books. Publishers will assist in setting up book signings and newspaper, television and radio interviews. An author shouldn't expect to be flown across the country for the interviews. The author more than likely will be interviewed by phone than spend an evening in a posh New York hotel.

This doesn't mean authors can't plan and execute their own book tours. Out-of-town book stores, libraries, civic groups and public organizations welcome authors to stop and talk to members of their organizations even when the author is on a vacation. A portion of an author's expenses can usually be deducted from taxes as a business expense.

All of the marketing of a book is the responsibility of a self-published author. If an author contracts with a vanity press, an internet service for print-on-demand or utilizes some other type of self-publishing company, the author will become the promotions person, salesperson, business manager, shipping clerk, secretary, janitor and every other type of employee hired by a publishing house. Either the author does the work or pays a marketing service. I know of authors who like the control of self-publishing. They have 100 percent of control over the way their books are edited, designed and printed. They also have 100 percent of the business responsibilities, including marketing.

I'm an author and I write. That should be enough.

Being just a writer won't lead to book sales in today's world. The mindset of an author needs to be adjusted.

Authors need to develop new skills. Understanding the business side of publishing is the first step.

Publishing is a business and a business needs to make money to survive. Publishers need to pay employees, the rent, postage, taxes and utility bills the same as any other company. Making money in today's publishing climate is difficult. Take a look at the demise of many traditional publishers. So many have either vanished, merged or changed their business strategy to become quasi-vanity publishers.

Authors also like to be paid for their creative work but they are often at the bottom of the money distribution list.

The subject and substance of a book doesn't always ensure a work will be published. Just because an author and five close friends believe a book would be interesting, doesn't mean the book will be published. Books need to have a wide audience to be successful. Also, the next great American novel might not be published if a publishing company believes readers won't purchase the work. A writer friend took part in a seminar in New York City where prospective authors had a chance to pitch their books to agents and publishers. She believed she had a book of substance that was well researched and written. She didn't get a nibble from the publishers. The twins from a chewing gum television commercial did receive great interest from the publishers.

A number of questions have to be answered before a traditional publisher agrees to publish a book. How many copies of the book are expected to be sold? Who will purchase the book? What will be cost of producing the book? What price should be charged for the book? What will be the company's expected revenues? How many copies should be printed in the initial run? Should the publication be just an e-book? Will there be foreign sales?

Economics is a crucial determining factor in the world of traditional publishers. The same factors traditional publishing houses examine should be explored by self-publishing authors. Self-publish authors need funding to produce a book. A successful author needs to determine costs and have a realistic view of potential sales before launching a book venture. **NOTE TO AUTHORS:** The copies given to friends and family do not count as sales.

The fiscal bottom line is important to publishers and authors.

Successful businessman Carl Francis has drilled into my head that marketing is everything. Carl is a good friend and a marketing and image genius who is an adjunct professor and lecturer at **Drexel University's LeBow College of Business** in the school's internationally-ranked MBA programs.

Marketing is everything and a successful marketing plan begins once the book is conceived. For those with a traditional publishing house, the book must be marketed to the acquisition editor. Before the book is released, an author should be identifying the target audience and letting those potential book buyers that the book is about to be released.

BOOK TITLES AND COVERS ARE PART OF MARKETING

A book's title and book cover design are keys to marketing success. A great title can increase book sales and a poor one can doom a book's sales. I'm getting better with book titles but an author isn't always the best person to select a final title or design a cover.

Barricade Books Publisher Carole Stuart is excellent with titles and designs. My book *Pickett's Charge: The Untold Story* is a prime example. For Civil War and history buffs the book clearly is identified with the battle of Gettysburg. The book cover is bright blue. I had imagined the traditional looking Civil War book with an old painting reproduced or image of a Civil War soldier. I wasn't sure at first but the bright blue cover certainly stands out on book store shelves. Carole's vision was correct.

I was recently asked to take a look at the draft of a self-published book. I immediately had concerns about the cover. The title didn't convey anything about the subject of the book. There was no promotional material about the book on the front or back covers. The cover design was done by a friend of the author. I mentioned to the author that readers looking at the book at a store will have no clue about the subject. I suggested a marketing message should be included. I was pleased when I was given a copy of the released book. Information was added to the cover and now potential readers know the subject.

I did get a book title correct. I wrote a book on the American Revolution's battle of Brandywine, which took place on September 11, 1777, in Chadds Ford, Pennsylvania. The book took a number of years to research and write. During the summer of 2001, just before the horrific terrorist attacks in the United States, I was in London looking at British army and government records surrounding the British participation in the battle.

I pondered different titles for the book. The *Battle of Brandywine* was a possibility. I could have called the book *Brandywine* but a number of other books used Brandywine in its title and are connected to a Pennsylvania river. A number of famous people, including Washington and Lafayette, took part in the battle. They could have been used as part of the book's title.

After the attacks on 9/11, I contacted my publisher. I said the title of the book should be *September 11, 1777*. I didn't want any reference to the terrorism of 2001 but the September 11 date had a new meaning for Americans. The subtitle I suggested was way too long, but *September 11, 1777* was perfect for the main title of the book.

I worked with an author who was self-publishing a book. When he told me the title of his book, I cringed and politely pointed out he should rethink the title. The main title was *Part of the Parade*. Tell me what the book is about. Is it a circus parade? How about a Mummers' parade? The book's subject was the people behind the scenes working for the Philadelphia Phillies' organization during 2008. The Phillies won the World Series that year and the city held a parade for the team. The book was a great idea and profiled a number of wonderful people. I still disagree with the title.

If someone on the internet saw a book with the title *Part of the Parade*, would they know the book is about the Phillies' employees? Don't think so. The publisher was following a trend in Philadelphia sports books at the time by having a cutesy title. *Pouring Six Beers at a Time: And Other Stories from a Lifetime in Baseball* was one such title authored by a Phillies executive. At least this book had baseball in the subtitle.

One section of a book that is important to the author but not always to the reader is the acknowledgements. Everyone that contributes to a book deserves recognition. Books are not published without the assistance of a number of people. Researching and writing nonfiction books usually involves lots of help. I've spent many hours in libraries and historical societies looking through records and in each one I've been greatly aided by those working in the archives.

The acknowledgements section also has marketing value, if you haven't guessed. Those mentioned in the book might purchase a copy or at least spread the word about a book where they received credit. In this instance, the marketing value is secondary to the politeness of giving credit to those who have assisted an author's book.

Authors aren't trained to be superior salespeople or marketing masterminds. The business side of being an author, at times, may feel overwhelming. As with any other skill, an author will improve with experience. Marketing isn't brain surgery.

Authors need to change their mindsets. They must embrace the necessity of being a businessperson.

An Authors as Marketers Checklist

- ☑ Change your mindset

- ☑ Overcome shyness

- ☑ Be your own publicist

- ☑ Understand the business of publishing

- ☑ Understand the business of being an author

- ☑ Realize being an author is not enough to be successful

- ☑ Covers, titles and acknowledgements are marketing tools

Chapter 2

IN THIS CHAPTER:

- ✧ Being a starving artist
- ✧ Controlling expectations
- ✧ Reality checks

The business side of writing can be daunting, exhausting and at times discouraging. Authors shouldn't allow the stresses to damper their enthusiasm. A friend once told me that he awakes each morning and concentrates on the tasks he can accomplish. He doesn't dwell on factors outside of his control and obstacles don't drive him into a paralysis that stops him from accomplishments within his control. I add another component to my friend's mantra. I try to avoid destructive negative people. They will quickly drain your creative juices.

Chapter 2

Grandiose Author Expectations

"Do you mean don't people buy (books)? A little, a very little—not so much as I could wish. Writing books, unless one be a great genius—and even then!—is the last road to fortune."

~Author Henry James

A common complaint from authors and writers today is that they can't make a living writing. The number of paid writing assignments for newspapers and magazines are dwindling. The number of newspapers and magazines are decreasing, so that makes sense. Also, even though a great amount of content is needed for newsletters, websites and other publications, many outlets are unwilling to pay for the writing.

Writers lamenting the lack of pay is not new. American author Henry James wrote about an author decrying a lack of interest in books in his 1888 novel *The Aspern Papers.* James was not the only writer of his period to depict starving artists. Operas were even based on the concept.

BEING A STARVING ARTIST
IS NOT A NEW PHENOMENON

When I began my career as an author, I received a bit of friendly advice from a dear friend and newspaper colleague, Mary Anderson. She said, "You know, you will never become rich from writing books." Mary was correct, there are few patrons of the arts that support individual artists.

One person approached me at a book signing and stated I must be rolling in dough because of the number of books I've sold. Sorry, not so. I wish it were true. If you take gross sales of my publications, they easily exceed $1 million. As every successful business owner knows, it is the bottom line that counts, the net proceeds and not the gross sales.

So, an author needs to calculate all of his expenses, including purchasing books from a publisher or printer, paying for professional services such as editing and proofreading, marketing, travel, computers, internet costs and many other expenses before determining the amount of profit.

That profit can be pocket change.

Unless an author has a major best seller, pocket change might be an apt description of the author's profits. Most authors and artists I know, write and paint for the creative experience. They are driven to use their talents to create a work of art. The monetary remuneration is secondary. In other words, most authors don't write to become rich. Authors do hope to make enough money to survive.

Unfulfilled grandiose expectations can sour and kill an author's spirit fairly quickly. When I talk to an aspiring author, especially one who has not previously tried his hand at writing, I always try to control expectations without destroying the person's zeal for his project. Many fine reasons exist for writing a book that doesn't have anything to do with money. Recording a family history is an excellent motive to write a book.

Authors don't often embark on a project that could take years to complete unless they believe their books will be popular and successful. For the most part, authors believe their words could be transferred to the big screen for an epic movie. Preceding the movie premier, authors envision themselves being interviewed on television and National Public Radio and being wined and dined by the networks and national publications. This all takes place while collecting huge royalty checks and working on their next novel.

While the dreamed grandeur is possible to achieve, the

chances of becoming the reincarnation of a 1980s rock star are slim.

REALITY CHECK

To keep what is left of one's sanity, an author should start out with a reality checklist. A good way to begin is by determining the audience for a book. An author should look past the genre of a publication. I've written several Civil War books. There are thousands upon thousands of Civil War enthusiasts. Does that mean my book is going to be sold to every one of those American History fans? Of course not. Not everyone is interested in Pickett's Charge or Fort Delaware, the subjects of my books.

A Civil War book on the buttons used on Union officers' uniforms in 1863 will appeal only to a fraction of those interested in the Civil War. And yes, the minutia of buttons used during the Civil War has been written about. A small audience exists. Even subjects dealing with Gettysburg, the pivotal engagement of the war, don't guarantee success. During the 150th anniversary of the battle of Gettysburg I had one Pennsylvania publisher tell me he doubted that my Pickett's Charge book would even sell 500 copies because of the glut of books on Gettysburg that year. Thankfully, that publisher was wrong. The book sold 500 copies within several months of publication and is still selling copies.

Did I expect to sell a million copies of *Pickett's Charge?* No. Did I expect to sell more than 500? Yes.

An author expecting huge sales and not attaining them will be easily discouraged.

Movie deals are also part of the expectations of authors. Writers dream of the stars that will play the characters of their books. While movies and television shows are made from books, this isn't the norm. The movie business is vastly different from publishing and is more difficult to crack.

An author expecting a movie deal is likely to be disappointed.

Just because a movie isn't made from a book or a royalty check for millions isn't received, doesn't mean the author isn't a success. Authors need to be realistic about their expectations.

Authors also need to be realistic about the amount of work that goes into writing a book. As has been written in many variations in the past few centuries, "Easy reading requires hard writing."

BEING AN AUTHOR IS HARD WORK

I've had more than one writer approach me and tell me writing is hard work. They have had wonderful ideas for books. They soon find out that writing takes a lot of time and a lot of effort.

A common concern is, "I don't know how to start." There is no one answer to most questions about writing. Whatever works for the author is the best course. Some writers need to be thoroughly organized before beginning to write while others just jump into the writing. It's a personal decision. The same holds true for the best time for a person to write. It's personal. The best time for me is in the morning.

I've been asked to co-write books with other people. If I like the subject and the person, I might consider doing so and have co-authored such books. For the most part, I turn down those requests.

One offer I received I easily declined. The guy wanted me to do the research, write the book, find the publisher and do the promotion. When I said I wanted at least half of the royalties, he said no. He wanted almost all of the money because it was his story. The request came from a criminal in the federal witness protection program. Actually, the request came from the man's brother who had read my book *Jailing the Johnston Gang*. I couldn't actually meet the criminal since he was in the witness protection program. All of my communications with him were by e-mail. He was a police informer with a criminal record. He was also acquitted of murdering his girlfriend. He actually successfully used the defense of "I didn't know the gun was loaded."

The criminal had an unrealistic expectation of the whole process. He finally said he would write the book himself. He hasn't done so after many years.

Writing is hard work but that subject is for, well, another book. We're here to discuss marketing.

The business side of writing can be daunting, exhausting

and at times discouraging. Authors shouldn't allow the stresses to damper their enthusiasm. A friend once told me that he awakes each morning and concentrates on the tasks he can accomplish. He doesn't dwell on factors outside of his control and obstacles don't drive him into a paralysis that stops him from accomplishments within his control. I add another component to my friend's mantra. I try to avoid destructive negative people. They will quickly drain your creative juices.

At the end of the day, I've also found it is better to review your accomplishments than to look at the undone tasks facing you in the morning. Celebrate your daily achievements.

Grandiose Author Expectations Checklist

☑ Start with reasonable expectations

☑ Realize that getting rich is a long shot

☑ Starving artists are not a new phenomenon

☑ Do an honest reality check

☑ Don't be discouraged by marketing obstacles

☑ Valid reasons exist for writing a book other than money

☑ Writing is hard work

☑ Concentrate on your accomplishments

Chapter 3

IN THIS CHAPTER:

- ◇ Marketing begins early

- ◇ Self-promotion

- ◇ Preparing bios for marketing opportunities

- ◇ Press releases

- ◇ Relaxing because marketing isn't brain surgery

You can't judge a book by its cover but you certainly can lose sales with a poor one.

Chapter 3

Everything
Is Marketing

"Better three hours too soon than a minute too late."
~ William Shakespeare.

Quoting the Bard seems appropriate even though Shakespeare wasn't writing about marketing his work. An author who waits until after his book is published to begin marketing is way more than a minute late.

Everything is marketing. Carl Francis, a marketing and image professional, has told me so on several occasions. Authors seeking a traditional publisher start marketing when they approach publishers seeking a contract. Authors must sell their idea to the publisher. Who is going to buy the book? Why should you be the person to write the book?

Who is the audience? How are you going to sell your book? Those are common questions from publishers and they all are part of the marketing of a book.

MARKETING BEGINS EARLY

From the time I get an idea for a book, I begin thinking about the audience. Who will be the readers? I start making a list of individuals, organizations and groups. The information will be extremely important when I'm ready to contact a publisher and later when I begin sending out marketing information on my book. Authors don't want to be a minute late when the time for the book launch arrives.

The basic marketing process begins with the author. An author should develop a biography pointing out all relevant writing accomplishments. A highly praised paper from your grade school teacher on what you did on your family vacation doesn't count. Marketing the author is part of the process. I keep an updated bio that lists my writing career, number of books and the fact I've been featured on television and in print. That bio also includes contact information and a link to my website.

DON'T BE SHY

Many writers are shy about promoting themselves and their books. They need to get over their shyness. Authors need to be a shameless promotors. If an author doesn't self-promote, no one will.

Authors need to think about how they are presented to the public. If an author has a number of professions and identities, such as a scientist, business professional, writer, family man, and champion checkers player, he'll probably won't want to be known as the checkers king when he promotes his book on his latest scientific discovery.

Authors need good photographs of themselves for book covers and for use with internet marketing. Yes, authors need a good website and a social media presence. More on marketing through social media later in the book but having information on the author will be essential.

BOOK COVERS ARE ESSENTIAL TO MARKETING

Another early element of marketing is the look of the book's cover and the title. For self-published authors, this element is crucial. Traditional publishers usually have design teams to handle the layout of the cover and determine the title. The self-published author has to make the decision.

As mentioned earlier, the title needs to convey something to the reader. A generic title without a clue as to the content of the book doesn't work, especially if the cover has no other information. When a reader is browsing in a book store or scrolling online, the book title and design might be the only opportunity for an author to attract the reader's attention.

A book cover should help draw in the reader. The cover

is part of marketing. The book isn't selling the cover. The cover is selling the book. There is a difference and some artists might believe their creation should be the star and the book receive secondary billing. The cover design also must not be off-putting to the reader. Graphic depictions of murders shouldn't be used.

For example, I worked with a fine artist for a cover of my fiction book, *First Date Homicides*. The book is based in fact but is a murder mystery. The artist and I discussed the cover before she worked her magic. We agreed the cover was not to be too graphic or disturbing to the reader. You don't want to lose sales because the cover is in bad taste.

Another example is the cover of my book on the American Revolution battle of Brandywine. I wanted the cover to have the painting *Nation Makers* by Howard Pyle. Pyle created the painting on the battle of Brandywine more than 100 years ago. The painting is owned by the Brandywine River Museum. I worked with the executive director of that museum to secure the rights to have the painting on the cover. The museum reserved the right to review the final design of the cover. That was fine with me as I knew the museum didn't want the painting altered. No mustaches were allowed to be added to the brave troops of George Washington's army.

You can't judge a book by its cover but you certainly can lose sales with a poor one.

An author needs to have information ready to send out at a moment's notice if requested by a reporter, organization looking for a speaker or someone interested in purchasing a book. Much of the same information will be needed for press releases and internet and social media marketing.

BE PREPARED FOR MARKETING OPPORTUNITIES

An author should have good photographs of himself and the book cover. I use a jpeg format whenever possible. It is easy to transmit over the internet. Don't use blurry photos. I gather photographs from signings to use on social media. Sometimes people will send me a photograph that isn't sharp. I thank those sending me images but I don't use all of them. Having a variety of good photographs helps marketing. An author doesn't want to use the same photograph all of the time.

For press releases, an author should remember to answer all of the basic journalistic questions: Who? What? Where? When? Why?

Essential information for releases includes the full name of the author and the book, contact information for reporters to schedule interviews and have questions answered, the price of the book and how a reader can purchase the book.

We're just getting started.

The "why" is an important part of the press release. Are you writing the press release because the book has just been released, a signing has been scheduled, a talk is to be given, a second printing has taken place, or some other reason? An author needs a reason to send a press release. Press releases that just say an author has a book won't gain traction. A newspaper doesn't print the same information in the headline and the opening paragraph but an author should do so in the release. The headline and opening sentence should contain the information an author wants the editor and reading public to know and understand.

Hit editors, readers, and reporters over the head with the most important information.

Hitting an editor over the head is allowed but an author shouldn't be a pest. Authors calling editors every day to see when a press release will be published won't be kindly treated and the press release might never see the light of day.

In my press releases, I try to include upcoming talks and signings I have scheduled. I also include a paragraph that has biographical information about myself and where I can be contacted.

This is what I use at the moment:

> Bruce E. Mowday is an award-winning author and newspaper reporter. He has authored more than 15 books on history, sports, business and true crime. Mowday has appeared on the *Discovery ID* channel, *C-SPAN*, the *Pennsylvania Cable Network* and Philadelphia and local television shows. He is a contributing editor with *Business 2 Business*

magazine. Mowday has hosted his own radio shows and was chairman of the Chester County Historical Society and president of the Brandywine Battlefield Park Associates. He is a board member of the Valley Forge Park Alliance and the Chester County Conference and Visitors Bureau. He is a frequent speaker at various civic and historical groups. For more information on Mowday, his books and his schedule of events, see *www.mowday.com.*

The information works for press releases and also for introductions for talks I give. The description is also on my website.

An author should look for valid reasons to write a press release and post information on social media. Again, don't expect publishers to do so. One of my first books for Arcadia Publishing sold out of the first printing in weeks. I requested my editor to write a release saying so. My request was declined. The publishing company didn't want to write a release on one author in fear of offending other authors or being deluged by requests for releases. I understood the company's position. I wrote my own release about the first printing selling out.

I didn't need the publisher's permission to write the release.

Authors should relax. Marketing isn't brain surgery.

Marketing Checklist

- ☑ Authors are marketers
- ☑ Marketing is everything
- ☑ Start marketing early
- ☑ Marketing and writing entails hard work
- ☑ Don't be shy
- ☑ Be a self-promotor
- ☑ Have photographs and complete biographical information
- ☑ Send complete press releases
- ☑ Be self-reliant
- ☑ Relax, marketing isn't brain surgery

Chapter 4

IN THIS CHAPTER:

- ✧ Promotional copies
- ✧ Setting the price of a book
- ✧ Legal and tax help
- ✧ Controlling book inventories
- ✧ Being prepared for signings
- ✧ Cash, checks, credit cards and credit

All contracts should be closely scrutinized by authors and reviewed by an attorney retained by the author. Attorneys can make sure authors are receiving a fair deal. Attorneys can also make sure authors are kept out of legal difficulties.

Chapter 4

Business Basics

Free books, paintings and Lamborghinis.

One of the first business lessons I learned as an author was that I shouldn't give away the store—that is freely hand out copies of my books without receiving compensation. I was hosting a radio show in West Chester, Pennsylvania, when the station manager expressed a great interest in my new book. I would have given him a copy but he told me authors should never give away free books. I'm going to contradict his blanket advice later in this chapter.

Authors love to have people read their books. The same goes for artists who love to have people admire their creations. An artist friend of mine told me she would like to give those adoring fans her work. Giving away books and paintings is an easy path to gain fans. Supplying free books and paintings is also the path to the poor house. You don't see any Lamborghini dealerships giving away cars to admirers, especially with the vehicle's starting list price of $399,500 for a new model.

Now let's challenge the radio station manager's blanket statement of never giving away copies. There are times dispensing free copies make perfect marketing sense. For authors with traditional publishers, the publishing house usually furnishes marketing copies to reviewers, book contests and other marketing entities. If you are a self-publisher, you need to decide how many books to give away. You need to keep in mind each book costs you money and weigh the cost against the perceived benefit. If an organization with thousands of members and potential book buyers request a free copy for a review in the organization's newsletter, then that free copy is a good investment. If a person who does a review for his own blog without any followers, you might not want to give out a copy.

PROMOTIONAL BOOK GIVEAWAYS

I've landed interviews on television and radio stations after giving out free copies to staff members. Getting before a large audience enhances the chance of sales. I remember being interviewed on the Pennsylvania Cable Network after my book *Jailing the Johnston Gang* was released. The review copy was in the hands of the interviewer and he had a number of post-it markers on pages and a long list of questions. This was a great use of a free book.

I have no problem in giving out a free copy to someone

who has offered substantial input into the creation of a book. You want them to be proud of your book. Chances are they will purchase additional copies or their friends and family will do so.

Often, I'm asked to donate a book for a silent auction for a charity. I almost always do so. The book is part of my marketing expense and the book will help raise money for a worthwhile cause.

Self-published authors should realize that not every book you have printed will be sold for a profit. If you print 500 copies and sell them at $20.00 per book, don't expect to gross $10,000.

You have to deduct the books that are used for marketing purposes. If you sell books on consignment at book stores or other types of shops, the stores will want a portion of the sales. Stores request different percentages. One store asked for 50 percent of the list price. That means an author will receive $10.00 per book on a $20.00 book. Careful, authors can lose money on each book sold if the discount is too high.

Store owners are not non-profit centers.

Store owners have expenses, such as rent, lights, salaries and books take up space that could be used for other items to sell. The store owners deserve some of the profits. They also have a clientele that the author doesn't have to chase.

One of my books I helped research and write was for a historical society. They were using the book as a legacy piece and also to raise funds for the society. They were selling the book for $25. They weren't giving stores a percentage of the sales. Few local stores stocked the books. The historical society wanted to know why I didn't sell the book when I did my signings and talks. They were willing to sell me books only at full price. That would mean I would do marketing and sales and not receive any compensation. That was an easy business decision. Nope, not worth my time and efforts.

SETTING THE PRICE OF THE BOOK

Speaking of the cost of the book, how is the price set? If you are working with a traditional publisher, the publisher will establish the price. A self-published author will make that determination. You don't want to price the book too high and have no one purchase the book. You also don't want to price the book too low and not be able to cover the cost of the production of the book. Taken into account must be the editing, proofreading, printing and marketing costs. Also, remember book stores take a percentage. Setting a price can make or break a self-publishing author.

Traditional publishers must make a profit, cover the cost of the book's production and marketing and cover the costs of the book seller and book distributor. That's the reason the author doesn't make much money on royalties from book sales. Most book contracts call for a percentage of the net sales—not the gross. Sometimes authors receive a predetermined amount of money for each book sold.

Shrewd authors should do a little negotiating when they are offered a standard contract. A majority of the cost of the production of a book is incurred in the first printing. Additional printings don't cost as much as design and editing costs are eliminated. Authors should ask for an increased percentage of royalties once a certain amount of books have been sold.

AUTHORS NEED PROFESSIONAL HELP

Authors need to know and understand their contracts with publishers. Authors shouldn't think they are going to take their books to bookstores and sell them directly to the stores. Contracts usually forbid that activity. Publishers and distributors make their money by selling to stores. Now, self-published authors need to sell directly to bookstore owners. Those self-published authors need to realize some book stores don't stock self-published authors because the quality of self-published books greatly vary. Also, book stores want to make sure books can be returned if they don't sell. Distributors accept returned books and they are placed back in the publisher's stock. Many self-published authors won't take back books or place them on consignment.

All contracts should be closely scrutinized by authors and reviewed by an attorney retained by the author. Attorneys can make sure authors are receiving a fair deal. Attorneys can also make sure authors are kept out of legal difficulties.

Speaking about keeping out of trouble, authors needed to remember the tax man cometh.

Authors need to adhere to the tax laws of their states and collect and remit sales tax where legally bound to do so. Also, book sales are considered income and need to be reported on income tax returns. Remember deductions can also be taken to offset income. Authors should keep receipts for any fees connected with writing, publishing and promoting.

Besides having a good attorney, authors need a good accountant. I run my book business out of my corporation, which means multiple tax filings with federal, state and local governmental entities. Robert Kratz, my accountant, saves me a lot of time and headaches by taking care of all of the filings to the federal, state and local tax agencies. I don't just dump a box of receipts on Robert's desk on April 15. I use a computer program to keep track of my company's expenses during the year and my accounting "books" are checked by accountants several times during the year.

An author will need a little space to keep the receipts for the year but a much larger space to store books. True, an author using print-on-demand books can order in small batches and e-books take up no space. All authors should have some books when giving a talk or having a book signing event. Readers want authors to sign their books. You can't do so on an e-book.

BOOK INVENTORIES

Where do you store books? How many should an author have on hand? I hate to sell out of books when I'm at an event. Sounds silly but when I run out of books it means I miscalculated the number of books I needed that day. I could have sold more books. A perfect sales day would be returning home with one copy of each title I took to the signing.

I usually keep enough books on hand for all of the events I have scheduled in the coming month. I keep a running inventory so I know when I'm running low on a book and need to reorder from a publisher. An author shouldn't wait until too close to an event to order books. I can usually receive books within five working days of placing an order, but there are times when books take a lot longer to deliver. Sometimes publishers and distributors won't have books to ship to me. Sometimes publishers are in the midst of reprinting my titles. Sometimes the books are delayed in shipping. There are many reasons for shipments not arriving in a timely fashion. That is why I try to give myself at least a month's cushion.

Authors should also keep an eye on a publisher's inventory. I frequently ask for a publisher to order another printing if I discover the publisher has few copies of my book in the warehouse. Many publishers don't print a large number of books at one time. They also don't want to have a lot of books sitting around the warehouse collecting dust.

Authors need to make sure books are stored on a dry place. Books kept in a damp cellar won't be sellable and the author will lose money. Speaking of dampness, an author should check the weather report if at an outside event. Don't store books on damp ground. Authors should carry a tarp to cover books if an unexpected rain storm takes place. Many authors also use a tent to keep themselves dry and out of the way of the hot sun.

Transporting books can injure an author's back if proper precautions aren't taken. Authors will need to take books stored at home to their vehicle and then take them into an event. All unsold books must then follow the reverse path. Boxes of books should be light enough to carry without injury. I use a small, old folding luggage carrier to transport books from my car to the event. By the way, when I traded a sports car for my Mitsubishi Outlander Sport, the loading and unloading of books became easier because I didn't have to lift the boxes out of a trunk that was lower than the trunk door. The Outlander Sport design allows me to slide the boxes in and out of the trunk.

When I agree to take part in an event, I try to find out the expected attendance and then select the titles and number of books I will take with me. For me, two boxes of books usually will cover what I need. If I can sell a third of the expected audience, I'm happy. When giving talks couples often attend and that cuts potential sales in half. Some people may already have a book and some are just not interested. My little luggage carrier is fine for two boxes and I can make three boxes work. An author doesn't want to lug individual boxes from a far parking lot to a venue, so some type of carrier is essential.

Part of the business basics is having all of the material you need for a signing available at all times. An author, of course, needs books and the pens to sign the books. I use the non-smear fine point Sharpie pens. Some authors use special pens. Any type of pen is fine but make sure the ink doesn't smear.

A table and tablecloth will be needed to display books and marketing material. Book stands allow customers to easily see covers of books. I suggest a decent sized table. I need the space for my multiple titles but an author with one book can fill a lot of space with copies of the book and promotional material. Authors need chairs to sit during the signing session. I take two as I enjoying having people sit and talk during the events. Also, if an author gets hungry or need to use the rest rooms, it is good to have someone watch your table. Food and water, or other liquids, are needed for an outside event.

CASH, CHECKS, CREDITS CARDS, AND CREDIT

People don't always have the correct amount of money for books, so authors need to have to have some change available. I usually have at least a dozen $1 bills when I attend events and $5, $10 and $20 bills available. At least twice a year, the first person to purchase a book will only have a $100 bill. I don't turn away the sale. Also, I try to adjust the cost of my books to make sure I don't have to deal with coins. For the books priced $19.99, I'll tell buyers the cost is $20 and that I make my millions on the extra penny. I haven't found anyone to object, especially if I'm running some type of incentive for purchasing a specific book or multiple books.

An author will have to determine if he will accept checks and credit cards. I suggest getting a Square for credit cards. The cost to the author for using Square is minimal and I've noticed my sales have increased since I've used the device. I also accept checks and never have had one bounce. Well, I did once and the person was mortified. The woman's checking account was closed and a new one opened and she used a check from the old account. She made good the check.

I find a vast majority of people are honest and I trust them.

I've had many instances where people wanted a book but didn't have cash, a check or a credit card. Do you turn them away? In a majority of cases I don't. I offer them a chance to send me a check when they return home. Most of the people take me up on this offer and are pleased that I trusted them. Many people insist on giving me their names and contact information. You know they are trustworthy people.

Have I ever not received a check? Yes, only twice in the hundreds of times that I've trusted a person to forward a check to me. The first instance was a family at a historical event. I believe they lost my contact information. The second one was at a talk at a Unitarian Church event. I'm not sure why the man didn't send me a check.

How do readers know to contact me and where to send the check? The answer is part of my marketing material. I use a bookmark that says signed by the author. The bookmark includes my photo, name, contact information, website address, e-mail address, snail-mail address and telephone number. The information on the bookmark also allows readers to contact me to purchase additional books and to schedule me for my speaking services.

A Business Basics Checklist

- ☑ Set price of book to succeed
- ☑ Remit taxes due
- ☑ Have a good attorney
- ☑ Have a good accountant
- ☑ Know when to provide free promotional copies of books.
- ☑ Manage book inventory
- ☑ Accept credit cards
- ☑ Have a credit policy
- ☑ For signings and talks have:
- ☑ A sufficient supply of books

- ☑ A table and tablecloth
- ☑ Book stands
- ☑ Chairs
- ☑ Tarp
- ☑ Marketing material
- ☑ Non-smear pens
- ☑ Tent
- ☑ Money for change
- ☑ A way to transport books
- ☑ Contact information for patrons

Getting Published Seminar

Date: 10/26/2013

Time: 9:00 am to 11:30 am

Registration and Coffee at 8:30 am

The Oxford Public Library is hosting a book publishing seminar featuring authors Bruce Mowday and Ray Sarnacki. This seminar is for those writing books and seeking a publisher, published authors and those interested in the publishing industry. The cost is $50 per person. Call the library or register online at www.oxfordpubliclibrary.org

Contact person: Oxford Library
610-932-9625

BRUCE MOWDAY

The National Iron & Steel Heritage Museum
HISTORY LECTURE SERIES

Bruce Mowday:
**Defending Picket's Charge:
150th Anniversary of the
Battle of Gettysburg**

MAY 2, 2013 | 6-8 PM

Pickett's Charge Coatesville Talk

*Chester County
Library Sign*

*Johnston Gang
Poster*

Bookcover

Bruce at Kennett Library

Town of Chesapeake Beach
rs and Stripes Festival
onoring Our Fallen Heroes
May 28 – 30, 2016
www.chesapeake-beach.md.us

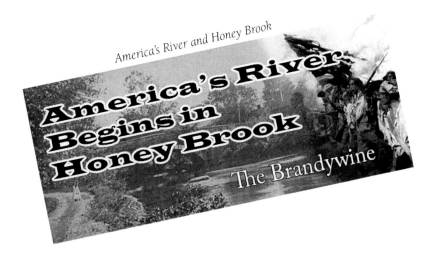

Wine & Words

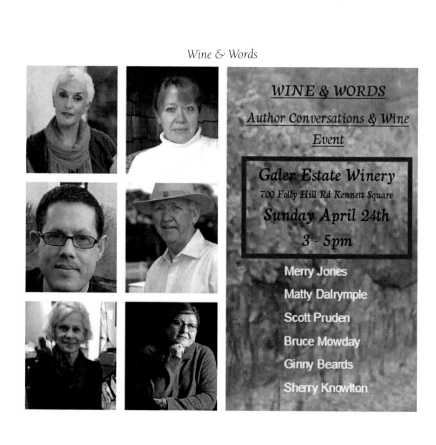

WINE & WORDS

Author Conversations & Wine
Event

Galer Estate Winery
700 Folly Hill Rd Kennett Square
Sunday April 24th
3 - 5pm

Merry Jones

Matty Dalrymple

Scott Pruden

Bruce Mowday

Ginny Beards

Sherry Knowlton

TO KICK-OFF THE AWARD NOMINATION PERIOD
THE WEST CHESTER DOWNTOWN FOUNDATION

presents

A LECTURE BY CHESTER COUNTY AUTHOR

Bruce E. Mowday

Award winning author, editor and newspaper reporter, Bruce Mowday will talk about the rich history of West Chester. Bruce is the author of 16 books including *Six Walking Tours of West Chester*. He will also preview his new book.

MONDAY, APRIL 11, 2016

6:00pm

SIDE BAR & RESTAURANT
10 E GAY ST, WEST CHESTER, PA   *a free event*

WC PRESERVATION AWARDS
Elevating appreciation of West Chester's
rich character and encouraging the preservation
of its historic integrity.

Save the Date – WC PRESERVATION AWARDS CEREMONY
THURSDAY, OCTOBER 20, 2016 *5:30 pm at* CHESTER COUNTY HISTORICAL SOCIETY

Contact David Reinfeld for sponsorship information - dreinfeld@chestercohistorical.org

Nominations accepted April 11 to June 10. To learn more and to apply for consideration please visit
DOWNTOWNWESTCHESTER.COM *or* **FACEBOOK**

Bar Association Esq.

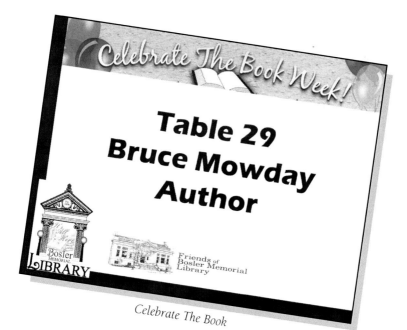

Celebrate The Book

Bruce & Rosie Ranck Wegman

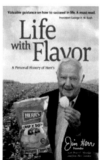

Chapter 5

IN THIS CHAPTER:

- ✧ Meeting the public
- ✧ Engaging the public; rejection
- ✧ Being positive
- ✧ Preparing a book talk
- ✧ Being an entertainer
- ✧ Knowing your audience

An author needs to be ready to engage a reader and get him interested in his book. Authors won't have a great amount of time, a minute or so if an author is lucky, I have developed a statement I use for each book — an elevator speech if you will — when I'm engaging someone. When I notice a reader reacting to one of points, I'll stop and add more information on the subject. One of my goals is to get a book into the hands of the reader. The act of holding a book many times leads to a sale.

Chapter 5

Meeting the Public

Shyness is not an option.

Writing is a lonely profession and being shy isn't a disadvantage. For an author marketing his books, shyness is a pronounced disadvantage.

To be successful, authors need to engage the public. Some of the meetings will be on the internet where it will be easier for the shy writer to make contact with readers. Some engagements will be in person where an author needs to abandon shyness.

If you check the internet, you'll find a number of articles that deal with eliminating shyness. An author needs to be brave and step into the public arena. The first public event will be scary but the trauma will subside as an author takes part in public events. An author will learn to survive.

Remember, authors are their own best salespersons. Friends, relatives and fans can help you increase sales but an author is the main salesperson. The first sales to friends and family are easy. Selling to strangers is the challenge. If an author isn't enthusiastic about promoting his book, no one else will be either.

ENGAGE THE PUBLIC

When attending a book signing, authors need to engage the public. They shouldn't sit on chairs and stare into space. Authors should make eye contact and attempt to start a conversation with potential readers. Some people won't want to talk to authors or will rush by their tables. That is fine. Don't chase them down and force a book into their hands.

Authors shouldn't worry about the rejection. Not everyone is going to purchase a book. In fact, only a small percentage of the populace will buy an author's book. Several studies indicate the average sale of a book is less than 200 copies.

Not every person stopping at an author's table is thinking about purchasing a book. They might want to know where the bathrooms are located or the path to the café. At one of the Barnes & Noble stores where I do a number of signings, I also know where the help desk is and some of the topic sections. I've been asked if I work at the store.

An author also needs to be positive. My first book was on the Civil War and one of my first signings was scheduled at Gettysburg National Park. Other authors from the same publishing company were there for a weekend of signings at various locations. At the first signing I was paired with another author who was mad about his book. He complained about the cover illustration, the title and just about every other aspect of the book. I kept my distance from him. I stayed at one end of the table and reached out to visitors. He sat in his chair with arms crossed across the desk at the other end of the table. He didn't need a "Don't Approach Me" sign. His negativity didn't garner him any sales. By the end of the weekend, the disgruntled author had changed his tactics. A member of publishing house told me that the disgruntled author observed my marketing technique and decided if he was going to sell any books he had to copy my lead.

An author needs to be ready to engage a reader and get him interested in his book. Authors won't have a great amount of time, a minute or so if an author is lucky, I have developed a statement I use for each book—an elevator speech if you will—when I'm engaging someone. When I notice a reader reacting to one of points, I'll stop and add more information on the subject. One of my goals is to get a book into the hands of the reader. The act of holding a book many times leads to a sale.

With experience, an author can tell if those stopping are interested in purchasing a book, wanting to engage in conversation or just looking for a place to stand for a time. I've had such people hang around my table for a good part of a day without saying much. As long as they aren't interfering with customers interested in my books, I don't mind.

When I interviewed successful businessman Jim Herr of Herr Foods for my book *Life With Flavor*, he said he always treated people the way he wanted to be treated. Besides being a success in business, Jim was a wonderful person. He had another personal rule. He said when he made a promise, he kept it. Authors should abide by the Herr rules, keep your word and treat people like you want to be treated. A friend of mine told me he had an opportunity to meet a well-known writer and he was looking forward to having an opportunity to privately talk to the man. The writer was not a nice person and I doubt my friend has purchased another one of his books.

Being a speaker for organizations, civic clubs and other groups is one of the most successful ways I have to market my books. An author's shyness must be hidden away in a corner for a few hours. Yes, I said hours, not minutes.

When I have a speaking engagement, I like to arrive early. I display my books and meet people. A sale of a book can be the result of a reader having a few minutes with the author. I also like to learn a little about the dynamics of the group before I give my talk. At one Rotary talk at a breakfast meeting, I sat with three men, all named David. Usually, only men named David are allowed at the table. Obviously, they liked to have fun. During breakfast we talked about my book and I mentioned I did some research at the David Library in Pennsylvania. They told me to make sure I mentioned the David Library during my talk. They said when I did so they would stand up and cheer the David reference. I did so. They did. The club members groaned and then laughed. I sold a lot of books that morning.

PREPARE TALKS FOR BOOKS

An author needs to have different versions of a talk about a book. For most of the service clubs, especially ones with breakfast or lunch meetings, the talk will last 15 or 20 minutes and then a few minutes for questions. The members are usually business people and need to go back to work. For night meetings and after dinner talks, the length needs to be from 30 minutes to an hour, depending on the group. I always ask how long a group wants me to speak and try to stay close to the time allotted. I've had groups that are so engaged in a topic that I'm told to keep going. An author needs to have some extra information handy for such occasions.

The first time I give a talk on a new book is always the most difficult. I spend a good amount of time preparing the initial talk. I usually do a quick outline and then write out the whole speech. I'll then do several readings to myself and adjust language as needed. Before giving the speech I'll read it to myself several times and at least try to memorize the flow of the talk. Authors shouldn't worry about reading the exact words on the paper. I tell people I never give the exact same speech. I'll adjust some talks to the subjects that I believe the group are interested in hearing.

I take the written script of the speech with me the first time I give a talk but I try not to read from the paper.

I highlight a few phrases and glance down at the paper from time to time to remind myself of points I want to make during the talk. I like to keep eye contact with the audience as much as possible. I walk back and forth at the front of the room. I have to be careful because one time I almost walked off a stage. Another time a person told me the roaming was too distracting for him. I find I can keep the attention of people by doing so, especially during an hour's presentation.

Personally, I don't like Power Point presentations. Those in the audience concentrate on the slides on the screen and not what you're telling them. The slides can be distracting. If the slides aren't clear—I've seen some authors use slides that are indecipherable—or the equipment doesn't work, the author is in trouble. After a meal, people can doze off in the soft glow of the Power Point.

BE AN ENTERTAINER

Authors need to be entertainers. The audience needs to be engaged. A caution, don't tell jokes. They hardly ever work.

The second or third time I give the same talk I usually don't bother with the written notes. As I stated, I don't give the exact same talk every time. Authors should make sure the information given to an audience is correct. If you are asked a question and you don't know the answer, say so. Don't guess. An author needs to be honest with an audience. Early in my career as an author marketer I gave a talk to a history group. An older man was convinced he was right about an incorrect fact. I didn't want to hurt the man's feelings and I didn't correct his misinformation. A member of the audience later asked me about the incorrect information. By not wanting to hurt the man's feelings, it lessened my credibility before the group. I haven't made that mistake again.

KNOW YOUR AUDIENCE

An author never knows who is in the audience. Experts on an author's subject, or people who think they are experts, could be attending a talk. The latter ones can cause issues. An author doesn't want to fight with people in the audience. An author should learn tactics to graciously change the subject and continue with the talk or questions.

I gave a talk at the Chester County Historical Society about Mark Sullivan, noted newspaper writer and national magazine correspondent who lived in the early 1900s. I had authored a newspaper article on Sullivan and the historical society wanted me to give a talk since Sullivan was from Chester County. I discovered that several people in the audience knew Sullivan. I encouraged them to give personal experiences about Sullivan and their input helped the talk.

I've given quite a number of talks on my true crime book, *Jailing the Johnston Gang: Bringing Serial Murderers to Justice*. True crime is a favorite topic of groups, especially if the crime took place in the organization's immediate area. During a talk at a library, I arrived early and discovered in the audience was a family member of a murder victim and a family member of the person that killed him. I didn't let on who they were and they never made the connection. For the same book at a different talk, a young man thanked me for writing the book. When I asked why, the young man said he was a youngster when his father was murdered and the book answered some of the questions about his death. At my first talk about the book a woman sat directly in front of me and she obviously was upset. I found out the woman was the mother of another murder victim.

You don't know who may be in the audience.

When giving talks on books, authors should not tell everything in the book. If an author does so, readers will have little reason to purchase a book. Readers want to know about the author, where the author got the idea for the book and the process of writing the book. Authors are the stars along with their books at signings.

Authors owe their best effort to those who have gathered to hear talks, even when the author is sick or distracted by life issues. I've had readers travel fairly long distances to hear talks and braved foul weather.

The show must go on.

Meeting The Public Checklist

- ☑ Shyness is not an option
- ☑ You are the top salesman
- ☑ Be positive
- ☑ Prepare book talks
- ☑ Be an entertainer
- ☑ Have a story to tell
- ☑ Engage audiences
- ☑ Know your audience

Chapter 6

IN THIS CHAPTER:

- ✧ Utilizing social media

- ✧ Budget advertising dollars

- ✧ Competition

- ✧ Websites

- ✧ Rethinking platforms

- ✧ Experimenting with marketing campaigns

- ✧ Working with other writers

Paid advertising can be expensive and decimate a marketing budget without boosting the bottom line. I remember a discussion with a newspaper salesperson who wanted me to take out an ad for one of my books. There was a special section being printed and I could have had a nice sized ad for about $500. What a deal! Let's see, if people seeing the ad went to the internet and ordered my book, I would have to sell more than 200 books just to break even. The newspaper salesman could not guarantee those sales. I didn't purchase the ad.

Chapter 6

Social Media

The best of times and the worst of times.

Social media has created the best of times and worst of times for authors. (I apologize to Charles Dickens.) An author not utilizing social media is not fully marketing books. An author mishandling social media wastes time and money.

In the good old days of the last century an author could successfully promote books by a multitude of ways. The author could hire a publicity agent, write press releases and distribute them to newspapers and magazines, drop by multiple book stores for signings and appear, if lucky, on radio and television shows. They were the good old days. Today, social media and the internet have drastically changed the field of marketing books.

Newspaper and magazines, especially newspapers, can't be relied upon to disseminate information about a book. Hometown newspapers were excellent at alerting the public to a new book by a local author. Newspapers are folding and consolidating, so fewer of them are available. The papers are not publishing as much local news and events, such as book signings. People are not reading the print version and the number of people paying close attention to internet newspapers is not great. An author relying just on newspapers won't reach many readers. That saying, don't dismiss newspapers. Authors should use every avenue for free publicity that is available.

USE MARKETING DOLLARS WISELY

Notice I used the word free. Paid advertising can be expensive and decimate a marketing budget without boosting the bottom line. I remember a discussion with a newspaper salesperson who wanted me to take out an ad for one of my books. There was a special section being printed and I could have had a nice sized ad for about $500. What a deal! Let's see, if people seeing the ad went to the internet and ordered my book, I would have to sell more than 200 books just to break even. The newspaper salesman could not guarantee those sales. I didn't purchase the ad.

The purchasing of the ad was not the best use of my marketing budget. By the way, authors considering paying for ads should find out the circulation of the publication, when the publication will be circulated and how the publication will be circulated. If an author is told a million copies will be printed, an author wants to make sure the copies aren't stored someplace and never distributed. An author of a book about the history of Camden, New Jersey, doesn't want to advertise in a publication being distributed in San Jose, California.

Paid public relation services need the same scrutiny. The payoff is in the number of books sold, not the number of news releases distributed. Editors like to see some local connection to press releases. A basic release sent to numerous outlets has little chance of being published. I know. I was an editor who sent them to an electronic trash can or a real trash can.

Specialty magazines can play a great role in marketing books. I write some books on history and when I write one on the Civil War there are many Civil War publications to market my book. Magazines in print and on the internet abound on fiction and non-fiction subjects. They should all be alerted and sent press releases and publishing information.

Before my first book was published, I went to bookstores and thought to myself that if all of those authors could have books published so could I. Later I went to the same bookstores and thought about all of the competition. Now I go to Amazon.com and the Barnes & Noble website and think how can anyone find a book on the internet? Amazon lists more than 11 million books. That's a lot of competition and the number grows each year. One book agency reported more than 1 million new books were printed in the United States in 2009.

Now, that's a lot of competition!

HAVE A WEBSITE

Authors need a website promoting their books. The website can act as the home base. I direct people interested in my books to my website. The website has all of my marketing material and information on ways to purchase my books and how to book me for a speaking engagement. My Facebook page is fine but I'd  rather have people on my website. The website needs to have fresh information added on a consistent basis.

I'm an author, not a programmer or a website developer. Spending time tinkering with websites is a waste of time for me. I go to the experts for assistance. Again, keep an eye on the costs. You don't want to spend tens of thousands of dollars on a website for one local book. Website design options are available at reasonable prices. I use a website where I can do updates myself. You don't want to pay have someone add information every other day. Every time I add a new speaking engagement or book signing, I update my website.

Being active in social media is a must for successful authors. Social media can reach readers economically better than any other marketing venture. Sites promote paid advertising to boost the number of people seeing an author's post, thus increasing the chances of making sales. Authors must set a budget for such paid advertising and target those receiving the postings. If an author is writing a history of Downingtown, Pennsylvania, making sure people in Miami, Florida, read about the book won't increase sales. The postings should go to people living in Downingtown.

STAY ABREAST OF SOCIAL MEDIA TRENDS

The world of social media changes rapidly and authors need to keep an eye on social media trends. New social media sites are added to the internet and become popular and other ones lose favor and die. Authors should be active on as many of the sites as they can.

Posting to social media isn't as time consuming as it appears. Photographs and copy for a subject can be written once and then posted to all social media sites. Don't reinvent the wheel every time. Some sites have word limits, Twitter for example. Sometimes I have to edit a posting I did for Facebook for Twitter. Sometimes I make two Twitter postings. It's not very time consuming.

Smart author marketers use information on the social media sites to help target readers interested in books. For my Civil War books, I can find groups interested in that time period of history. Most internet groups won't allow an ad for a book to be posted but there are ways to post information without being too obvious that it is marketing. If an author violates rules of the group too often, the author can be banned from posting.

Publishers pay attention to authors' platforms as a way to gauge the popularity of authors. Platforms can be very misleading. I had a conversation with a publisher about a book the company had high hopes of sales. The publisher was basing the sales on the author's followers. The sales were disappointing.

RETHINK USE OF PLATFORMS

Platforms include those readers following an author on social media. The followers can be friends on Facebook and other social media sites and followers of an author's blog or podcast. Not every post is read by every friend. In fact, about a third of posts are read. Some friends never read anything posted on social media sites. The same goes for "likes" on a page. An author can accumulate a lot of likes but never have a person return to the page. I'd rather have a friend share one of my postings. The friend is helping to disseminate my marketing to all of his friends.

Blogs by authors can be successful if they are constantly updated with fresh and interesting information. A lot of valuable time is taken away from writing and other marketing efforts in blog writing. Having one good idea a week for a blog is difficult when you think about the number of subjects needed for a year. Few bloggers can dazzle readers for such an extended period. I know. For a year I was a newspaper columnist and did three columns a week. Being a regular columnist was the most difficult assignment I had in my career as a newspaper reporter. If a blogger doesn't have excellent content, readers will not return to the blog. The same reasoning should be used for podcasts. To be successful, the content must of excellent and lots of them need to be done.

Instead of attracting and keeping platform friends, authors would be wiser to use existing networks already established on social media. Those communities stay together because of a common interest. Authors can add information on their books and writings to the established communities.

The internet and social media should be utilized to pinpoint groups seeking speakers. For the history books, a search of Civil War Round Tables is an excellent way begin marketing and seeking talks. If a group wants a copy of a book to review, send them a free copy. The group is a target audience.

Authors need to identify groups of readers and determine how to reach them. This can take some time but it is an effective method to schedule talks, signings and sell books. Authors waiting for groups to find them will have a long wait and few sales.

EXPERIMENT WITH MARKETING CAMPAIGNS

I experiment with different marketing approaches to discover ones that are successful. Some of the marketing experiments work and some don't. For one family history book I purchased a mailing list of persons with the family name and had postcards made and mailed. I didn't quite sell enough books to recoup my expenses. I've dropped the mailing approach. My first attempt to use just Facebook, no other marketing, to do a book talk and signing was successful. The event was held at an area restaurant connected to my book's historical event. I worked with the restaurant owner and picked a slow day. The restauranteur wanted more people in his establishment. We packed the dining room. The restauranteur was happy as he sold a number of meals that night. Meals were still being served when my talk began. That wasn't a problem. The restaurant owner didn't charge me for the venue, so that cut down on expenses. We didn't charge for admission so people were more apt to attend, dine and purchase books. I sold a number of copies that evening. That was a good partnership. I've since done talks and presentations at a number of restaurants.

There is one group on social media and the internet that authors spend too much time chasing. The group is authors. There is a great benefit to discussing common writing and publishing issues. I was one of the founding members of the Brandywine Valley Writers Group a number of years ago. Writers feel better socializing with other writers. Authors need to remember, other authors don't usually purchase books.

There is an author-related industry that I find distasteful and dishonest to readers. That industry involves authors paying to join a group so that other authors, who also have paid to join the group, will write favorable reviews of their books. Most readers don't realize a pay-to-review scam is taking place. To be honest, the reviews should say: "George Doe gave me a glowing review and it only cost me $500." All authors want and crave positive reviews and negative ones sting. I certainly promote comments from readers who like my books. Some readers rely on reviews but I don't trust them when I select a book.

A Social Media Checklist

- ☑ Be active on as many social media sites as possible
- ☑ Keep up-to-date on social media changes
- ☑ Use a well-designed website as your home base
- ☑ Provide fresh copy for website and social media sites on a consistent basis
- ☑ Evaluate use of platforms
- ☑ Use social media research tools to identify and contact readers
- ☑ Use social media to drive readers to talks and signings
- ☑ Budget social media marketing dollars
- ☑ Experiment with marketing campaigns

Chapter 7

IN THIS CHAPTER:

- ✧ Scheduling events
- ✧ Being available for signing and talks
- ✧ Working with bookstores
- ✧ Not being pushy
- ✧ Unusual venues
- ✧ Selling previously published books

There are times when organizations offer me options of when during the year I would like to talk. Many groups look for multiple speakers during the year. Given my choice, I'll load talks in November and early December rather than February when a snow storm is likely to keep everyone from a signing. Books make great gifts during the Christmas season. Authors should be extremely active during November and December.

Chapter 7

Converting Maketing
Into Sales

Hit the Road Jack.

Authors with books in hand are ready to hit the road and start making sales. Yes, I said get ready for road trips. An author sitting in his office behind a computer trying to make sales is ignoring the best way to sell books.

I've been accused of selling books out of the trunk of my car. That's not always so. I sometimes have them in the back seat.

Readers like to see and talk to authors. Readers attend signings and talks for many varied reasons. Some will like the topic of the book. Some people are fascinated with the writing process. Other people are budding authors and seek tips to make them successful. Authors need to engage readers.

AVOID CONFLICTS WHEN SCHEDULING SIGNINGS

The scheduling of signings and talks is important. An author doesn't want to schedule a book signing on Super Bowl Sunday or the night of the finale of a television program that has a huge audience. Authors need to be aware of conflicts that will keep people away from their events. Don't rely on organizations to take such notice. I recently had a historical group asking me to talk on an afternoon where multiple other larger community events were taking place. I declined the invitation and agreed to sign at one of the other venues.

One of the larger events I didn't attend was the Kennett Square, Pennsylvania, mushroom festival even though I've written a book about the mushroom industry. One year I did go to the festival. The event draws thousands of people. I discovered they were there to eat mushrooms and not to buy books. I decided to go to another local event with less attendance but many more book buyers. Authors need to try out different venues but keep a bottom line on sales.

New authors have a tendency to want to schedule as many signings as they can within their community when a book is released. That's good and bad. An author can reach many different readers in a community by appearing before different groups. If a number of book store signings is done within a few days, an author will discover sales dwindle with each succeeding signing since most book buyers will appear at the first one convenient to their schedules.

The most discouraging experience for an author is to appear for a signing and have no one there interested in your book. I remember my first book store signing and some people did attend. That evening I began to realize that I would have to put in a marketing effort to make book signings successful.

WORK WITH BOOK STORE PERSONNEL

Authors should work with book store personnel to promote signings. Authors shouldn't rely on book stores to do all of the marketing work. Also, authors need to remember when they are in the store they are there to sell books and not be pampered. Some of my book store contacts tell me of horror stories of demanding prima donna authors. They want to be waited upon and given lavish meals. The book store professionals are in the stores to sell books and not to wait on the authors. Demanding authors won't be asked back, that is unless they sell an extraordinary amount of books.

I also was told of one author's appearance that resulted in a fairly large audience for a book talk. The author talked and talked and talked and wouldn't stop even when the book store employee tried to stop the presentation. The crowd dwindled as the author talked and by the time the author ceased her presentation few people were left to buy books. Authors need to know when to be quiet and pick-up a signing pen.

There are times when organizations offer me options of when during the year I would like to talk. Many groups look for multiple speakers during the year. Given my choice, I'll load talks in November and early December rather than February when a snow storm is likely to keep everyone from a signing. Books make great gifts during the Christmas season. Authors should be extremely active during November and December.

I have an excellent relationship with the local Barnes & Noble store in Exton, Pennsylvania. I usually schedule at least three signings in the weeks and days leading up to Christmas. The store provides a table, chair and my books near the entrance to the store and make announcements alerting customers that I'm signing books. I'm low maintenance. They usually offer coffee, tea or water and I appreciate and usually accept. For the three hours or so I'm in the store, I greet patrons, tell them about my books and sign them for the patrons. I know the store's layout and often direct patrons to the rest rooms and café. I've been mistaken for a store employee.

DON'T BE PUSHY

During book store signings and ones at local organizations and events, I try to get a book into the hands of a prospective buyer. Once the book is in a person's possession the sale becomes more likely. Authors shouldn't be pushy and obnoxious. I know of an author who is banned from giving presentations at a service club because he tried to force every member of the club to buy his book.

When I finish a talk, I'll stand by my book table and welcome additional discussions and sell and sign books to those interested. Usually,  someone will ask me to speak at another organization where he belong.

Authors need to seek out sales on the internet, at book stores and while taking part in community events. Every sale is important. That is why I use the tag line One More Book on my e-mail signature. For business reasons, I would rather do signings and talks at my own venues rather than at book stores. I purchase books from the publisher and sell directly to the public. No book distributors or stores split the profit.

SEEK OUT UNUSUAL VENUES

Authors should also look for unique venues to sell books. Not all books are sold at bookstores. I did a pictorial history of Coatesville, Pennsylvania, with a national history publisher. One of my venues was a local flower shop. I sold hundreds of copies of the book at the flower shop. People shopping for flowers for family events purchased the history book of the town.

If an author writes a book on NASCAR or some other automobile topic, the author should approach garages, car dealerships, auto parts stores or other such venues to sell his book. If an author writes a book on crocheting or other needle work subject, he should place the books in stores that sells such items and supplies. I have an author friend who writes such books and she is highly successful.

When determining the target group for a book, authors should realize a book can appeal to multiple groups. I've been working with Karl Kuerner, a noted artist taught by art legend Andrew Wyeth and his sister Carolyn. He's doing a series of landscapes of Gettysburg. This book will appeal to those who appreciate art, especially Andrew Wyeth fans, and to those who are interested in Gettysburg and the Civil War.

OLDER BOOKS SELL

When a new books is published, authors have an excellent opportunity to sell older titles. New titles mean new speaking engagements. Authors should take older books with them to the new venues.

Also, just because a book was published some years ago doesn't mean an author has to stop selling the book. When I give a talk on the Revolutionary War or the Civil War in a new area, most of those attending haven't seen my other historical books. The book is new to those readers. An author can sell previous books. One of my all-time top-selling books is on the American Revolution and published about 15 years ago. Last year I personally sold 100 copies of *September 11, 1777*, a book on the battle of Brandywine. If you add the number of books sold by stores and on the internet last year, that book published more than a decade ago sold more books last year than an average book sells in its lifetime.

A Sales Checklist

☑ Promote yourself

☑ Use non-traditional venues for talks and sales

☑ Be relentless

☑ Put books in the hands of readers

☑ Use talks to schedule additional talks

☑ Use new releases to sell previous titles

☑ Authors are the best salesmen

Chapter 8

IN THIS CHAPTER:

✧ Spending time with readers and the public

✧ Seeking out marketing opportunities

✧ Being an entrepreneur

When I was a newspaper reporter, I was always looking for a story. I was never not working as a reporter. My mother once refused to tell me a story about something that happened in the neighborhood because she was afraid I would write an article for my newspaper. I have the same mindset when it comes to book marketing.

Chapter 8

Final Words

One more book.

To successfully market books, authors need to spend time with the public and their readers. There is no way around meeting and greeting and interacting with the public. For me, I like giving presentations about my books. I tell the audiences my favorite part of the publishing process is talking with readers. And that's the truth, as Edith Ann used to say.

The world of book marketing is not for shy authors.

When I was a newspaper reporter, I was always looking for a story. I was never not working as a reporter. My mother once refused to tell me a story about something that happened in the neighborhood because she was afraid I would write an article for my newspaper. I have the same mindset when it comes to book marketing. Articles on the internet or printed in newspapers give me leads for marketing activities. If someone mentions they belong to an organization, I ask if they need speakers. If an organization is holding a community event, I see if it is feasible to spend a few hours selling books.

Authors need to be able to recognize marketing opportunities and to be willing to take advantage of the openings.

Authors need to be businessmen. Unless an author has a patron or isn't concerned about turning a profit, writing a book can be extremely expensive. I hear the same complaints from artists and musicians. Creating is time-consuming and not financially supported.

Authors shouldn't write just to sell books. I met an author in Gettysburg who asked me about my pending book projects. He said he churns out a book every six months. That was his business model. I wasn't sure about the quality of the research of his books. Some of my projects take three years or more to research and write. I know that I make way less than minimum wage if I look at what I earn per hour. Authors need to be proud of what they write.

Also, authors need to be able to perform many of the jobs done by publishing houses. Authors certainly need to be self-promoters. Authors can hire agents and publicists and some are highly successful with the professional help. Most authors don't sell enough books to make the hiring of such professionals economically feasible.

To sell one more book, authors need to be self-sufficient.

Authors are true entrepreneurs.

Index